PSYCHIC UNREST

Other works available by Lillian Allen

books
Women Do This Every Day (selected poems)
Nothing but a Hero (poetry for children and young people)
Why Me (children's book)

recordings
Conditions Critical (CD)
Freedom and Dance (CD)
Nothing but a Hero (tape for children and young people)
Revolutionary Tea Party (CD)

PSYCHIC UNREST

poetry by Lillian Allen

INSOMNIAC PRESS

Copyright © 1999 by Lillian Allen.

Some of these poems have previously appeared in various venues and versions. Several have been recorded on the CD *Freedom and Dance*. A version of "Poetry of Things" was recorded under the title "Poetry" with Roots Control on the CD. Live From the Planet Crooklyn by Word Sound I Powa and first appeared in print in CV^2. "Stereotype Friggin'" first appeared in print in *Fireweed* and "Mrs" in *Utterances & Incantations — Women, Poetry and Dub*.

Edited by Jill Battson.
Copy edited by Catherine Jenkins and Phlip Arima.
Designed by Mike O'Connor.

Canadian Cataloguing in Publication Data

Allen, Lillian, 1951-
   Psychic unrest

Poems
ISBN 1-895837-55-3

I. Title.

PS8551.L5554P79 1999   C811'.54   C99-931691-X
PR9199.3.A55P79 1999

The publisher gratefully acknowledges the support of the Canada Council and the Ontario Arts Council.

Printed and bound in Canada

Insomniac Press, 393 Shaw Street,
Toronto, Ontario, Canada, M6J 2X4
www.insomniacpress.com

The Canada Council | Le Conseil des Arts
FOR THE ARTS | DU CANADA
SINCE 1957 | DEPUIS 1957

ONTARIO ARTS COUNCIL
CONSEIL DES ARTS DE L'ONTARIO

*This collection is dedicated to
my dearest daughter Anta, now roaring into womanhood,
Sami and Aquon
And the memory of my dear friend, Liz Karlin.*

Special thanks — for being there
To some very important cultural touchstones:
Djanet Sears, Winsom, Lisa Steele, Nalo Hopkinson,
Sheron Fernandez, Clifton Joseph, Jamelie Hassan,
Buseje Bailey, Ashok Mathur and Motion.

And to Phyllis Gordon.

Thanks to Jill for her editorial support, Denise Maxwell for
her cover art and Gudrun Weaver for taking the time.

And I also wish to gratefully acknowledge the support of the
Toronto Arts Council.

Living in a state of psychic unrest, in a Borderland, is what makes poets write and artists create...

— Gloria Anzaldúa

How come history takes such a long time...

— Bruce Cockburn

Table of Contents

The Glory Of

ancestral flow of rhythmic lava
soul moments of minor greatness
and spiced alienation
fever thumps your veins
break tones and tongues
language astir atwist in tatters
split histories   body and spirit
libations ripple
give way to the soul's waterfall
the glory
sheer existence

The Poetry of Things

There is a place where no language goes
where fear is a door
where the mind comes to the edge of itself
reaches beyond
and finds itself where heartbeats are born
in the deep black comfort of life's passages
nothing to declare or defend
where infinity struggles to measure itself
in the perfect world of imperfection
the place from which poetry springs.

Everything well and wonderful is poetry.

The idea that through the creative imagination we can reorder our world and create a thing of enduring beauty is the essential idea of poetry.

All that is visionless and full of despair is wounded poetry.

Giving birth is the model for all new and revolutionary ideas. When we create a poem, we also give birth to new vibrations, new rhythms, new ways of seeing, new ways of knowing and new possibilities in the world. The work of the poet is that of midwife and birth mother.

Poets materialize something into our world that only existed before in sameness, or in fragments or sometimes in ugliness and in pain.

Writing poetry is work of the soul. Poetry is that dialogue between the world inside of us and the world outside.

Possibilities for poetry arise when the heart reaches and puts itself into words or brings itself into the existences of images.

Truth and beauty seek expression through the soul. The act of writing is also the act of naming; of calling into being Poetry brings into sharp focus the camera of one's mind's eye The poet sees with the soul.

The mind's eye sharpens and outlines. The soul reaches to pull focus, to grasp the essence of things, to resonate with that which vibrates most with beauty and truth.

Life is a way of being. Art is a way of seeing.

The essence of life is its possibilities. Possibilities arise with vision.

Life is inherently challenged to express itself beyond all possibilities.

That is the poetry of life.

We bring the intensity of poetry and creativity to our lives when we seek the essence of things — see possibilities in everything around us. We can laugh more often, weep more openly and seek to occupate the terrain of creativity and imagination as a right.

In the territory of the creative imagination
we connect the in and outside
touch notion of life
creativity
the creator self
; wellspring of touch
sparks between two fingertips
closeness of touch
the perfect world of imperfection

Such is the poetry of life

Everything well and wonderful is poetry.

Black Hips

handful of hot plastered rock
pluck on collar-bone
fingering strings
dancing bass groove
swish swash to the motion
footloose
riffs bellow blue notes
mesmerize counter-squeech
yelp of heaped-up vibrations
pulse trance
Black hips bump and grind
a grasp of what heaven or hell could
a story to tell

Strut

full-bodied cream and round browns
are snowflakes like chocolate
ready to melt all over your thighs
black blue steam is your breath
below circles of angels
sizzle asphalt on your tongue
rolled up double-step
like stretched rubber band reverberates
snapped at razor's edge
slices open the silence
splits apart language
sweetness and the thought
double time
strings slap to black heart wails
aches in arching beats
a rumble of syncopation
resolute
finally to exhale

So you want to write...? In whose language...?

OJ

Oh gee OJ
oh say can you see
I swear
I would never take a pen to OJ
pour out anger and fear
so generalized can't pinpoint
a direct source of spillage
only a silent scream that winds too deep
like a lost river
going back to places too ancient
for me to even remember
being woman and black.

Most times in america
we think confusion is clarity
as if anything can be as simple as CNN says

We have lost the authority of values in our lives
mettle batters against the rin dim din
persistent frenzy of peddled desires
where everything becomes
men in the starring roles
mostly a nightmare
being woman and black

Nothing is as complicated as those who must
and will not break the hypnosis
of US & them competition & greed politricks

Nothing can be as numbing as that silent
shade of power
that exalts itself by being omnipresent
and purposefully unindividualized

Nothing can be as terrible as being murdered
nothing can be as painful as losing a loved one
nothing can be as dread as poverty's noose
nothing is as ugly as racism
nothing is simple in a fucked-up America
being woman and black
with no relief in sight

The Wait of History

in the dawning of a golden day
in a schizophrenia
an alienation mushrooms

a river of hope
reality like a ghost
the snail pace of history

how could it be that no one goes to jail
for the crime Apartheid

we can forgive but not excuse
set in their old ways
pillage and privilege die hard
if not exorcised decisively

words of freedom
words of reconciliation
words words words
language is a militia

the sound of wait falls in the forest
the grey nothingness of appearances and systemics
a greater silence than prayer

in a schizophrenia
in the clanking rust slow turning wheels
equality is a bounced cheque
stamped justice
cash withdrawn by a few

The Broken of a Black Man

As if a great big wind would sweep
hello hello a haze
redundant   just a cold letter
loud conversations with himself
utterances and long sighs
disconnection   dread
closing in on him

Devour devour devour
like rage swallowing a flame
the intoxication of psalm ten
solace in hearing his own voice
the Almighty in his voice
bible clutched to his chest
like covering a wound

Sometimes he was afraid they beat him
charge him with something or other

Call the police call the police call the police
They called the police
disturbing the peace
his anguish desperate
they hated him
he read his Bible even louder   cursed them
flung his words like an MX missile or a Scud

They warned him to shut his fucking nigger mouth up
get his fucking Black self back where he came from
immigrant immigrant immigrant

After twenty-two years nine pairs of pants he wore
and no socks even in the devilish cold
redundant
cursed in Christie Pits

Shut up shut up shut up shut up niggah
systemic disturb
Shut up shut up
they hated him a Black man who wouldn't shut up
when he was told
redundant

They became his shadow
followed him home
he read his Bible even louder
disturbed
a free country Canada

Door slammed shut face of a shadow
thoughts slammed shut
he stood by his window sealed shut
smirking in his castle

brassiere

The policeman grimaced breath tightens
he hated the slamming and he hated
to see a Black man an immigrant looking
so smug
you're under arrest! — for what? — for jay walking, niggah!
careen shatters headlong sheen glass call an ambulance call
an ambulance call an ambulance
window splintering like thin panes of ice
against the policeman's service revolver
the broken home of the Black man

The Black man's hand pulled against glass
bones eeking against glass
jagged edges like ripsaw blade
dizzying flow of red
the Black man's world rapid shrinking to a dot

Call an ambulance call an ambulance
O Human Wrongs

O Human Wrongs

Three weeks later the Black man
able to leave the hospital
he went to the human rights commission
they said you again? His hand! how terrible how terrible eh
the four walls of his pain
system backed up on his back
would take two years or more

— 27 —

he already had two previous complaints against
clog up the system a cog in the system
Oh human wrongs

In her head a woman moves around without a telephone
the side of her face becoming swollen under her palm
a small child clings to her leg as if a great big wind

Sometimes she was afraid
sometimes she was afraid of him
sometimes she was afraid for him
and when she was afraid of him she called the police

The first police car came
the policeman who hated the slamming of the door
and hated to see a Black man an immigrant looking smug
ramboed into the house of the Black man
and then another police car arrived and then another and
then another and another
a cog backed up

The policeman pushed the woman out onto the veranda
before she could grab a hold of her young child
the earth exploded in her stomach
A neighbour runs to the scene   heard gunshots gunshots
terrible terrible terrible eh
The woman on the veranda no telephone hello hello

— 28 —

Through the window once made a weapon by the policeman
ramboed his way up the steps of the Black man's house
Sunday dinner splat rice and peas like children underfoot
the Black man a dot beside his aquamarine blue sofa

The young child clings to the mother leg's as if a great big wind
the world swirling to a dot
a sound from the vicinity of the young child's chest a bird's voice
they put my daddy to kneel
they put my daddy to kneel down beside the sofa and shoot him
they shoot my dadeee
daddy is still
my daddy isn't saying anything
I want my dadee   dadee
Call the police somebody the neighbour shouted will you.

Language

language is not just words
language is not just grammar
language is not just the English language

A Poem

You can never see a poem
as beautiful as a tree
for a poem is (but) a tree
in another dimension

Sapelo Island

the whisk of waves barely scented memories
angelic whispers in a dream
smooth fresh of ancient spirit connections
taste of longing for an ancestral womb
at the end of the middle passage
toes in the sands of history
Africa in your skin

highest register on the alto string of the cello
curls inside your ears
waves of magic light messages
silences that echo beyond history

arrival waves through tides of generation
splashes its lace-patterned foam
a bridal dress 'round an island
an end of a journeying five hundred years
from the shores of a mother

Fall Fall Falling

In a tempo of desert rain
rhythmic blues beat and gospel chants
love awakens

Wild bouquet's exquisite bloom
a lilting haunting scent
blues riffs running like a river
into the greens of ocean

In the early autumn sun near the cedar bench
sunlight shimmer bounce
tap-dancing shadows
curved underside stoneworked bridge

A lingering glow of summer catches your cheeks
and you can't stop smiling
something warm and secure you have sunk into

And there I am
quiet blissed and blessed
only childhood memories
hummingbirds' song
and sporadic moments of sprightly laughter
pull me back to rusting yellow leaves
on the orange earth

Cabretta Beach
(on Sapelo Island)

when the tides greet you
after the embrace
and the flushed cheek
eyelids flicker
glistening emerald waves
the shimmer of diamonds
like luminescent glitter of butterflies
a paradigm of endurance
for a people's survival
on pelicans' wings
blown and carried
to be found
like precious sand dollars of solid gold
on a magnificent beach
where God once stopped to pray

The myth of powerlessness is the TV of the masses

Contract on America

On news of the capture of suspect number one in the Oklahoma Bombing

They said he was a good soldier
he was kind to his cat
he once helped an old lady across the street
some say he was thoughtful
passionate with his views
when he ranted on about niggers and Jews
and blowing up those with differing views
they laughed their heads off ouh ouh ouh ouh
said 'boys will be boys'

Santa brought him another rifle for Christmas
made him recite his inalienable right
to keep and bear arms
to defend his fears

because he was too scared
to sit in a hot bath
light a candle
smell some incense
and let the world in

They said he was good with children
gentle and kind
he was like ...
                    well groomed
was like...
Like what? What did you expect?

Stereotype Friggin' — The Ethnic and the Visible Minority...in Stereo-Typed to Fit

A Greek young woman poet
explores her ethnicity
far from her roots
she explains by way of introduction
to a monologue
she was about to spring
that the racial slurs
contained therein
should not be taken as such
but seen in context
you know the saying
I'm not a racist...I'm not a racist...I'm not a racist...but
(I just sound like one...)

And not to be partial
she warned of her monotyped
Greek, immigranted no-speake-de-englise woman
chained in a monologue
impotent at the tip of the poet's pen

The poet's monologue unfurled
sliced the life of an immigranted ethnic
Greek woman
far from her roots

Downpressed, ethnic and Greek
the immigranted woman did the stereotyped thang
stayed at home cleaned

and sparkled everything
went to ESL
(because the social worker told her to)
met a feminist in women's clothing

Made song with those who were oppressed
dissatisfied with just regrets
but the immigranted woman being Greek and ethnic
dutiful took the beatings
her missing link husband served her up
(see how nicely this stereo fits the type)

And she endured
being Greek immigranted and ethnic
as if there was a medal
waiting to mark the years
as she spanokapekoed her days

And later she learned typing
to resist
that's how the feminist in women's clothing analyzed it

Certified at 30 words a clip-click
but her greek-englishe not so good
she went for a job
a friggin' mundane
type-friggin'-job
which she didn't get

(catch the clincher)
She didn't get the job
...because there was one single
type-friggin'-job to go around?
No!
She didn't get the job
because a visible minority
who couldn't type friggin'
was given the job.

So tonight at the church of employment equity
a visible minority woman worships
praises her God
a type friggin' job
she can't even type at
is delivered unto her

And those who set the interest rates
guard the gates
smugly safe
watch like a TV show
a situation comedic
if it weren't so tragic and strategic
as the Greek poetess
explores her ethnicity
far from the roots of any struggle
in Stereo... ooooooooo
Typed to Fit!!

Don't They Know

Elizabeth sits in the penitentiary
said it was self-defence
a war undeclared on women and children

Don't they know there's a war
there's a war going on down there
United Nations won't send no peacekeepers in
the Justice Department say its budget's thin

There are things words don't speak
rivers of tears don't stop the pain
regrets and speeches don't materialize change

Don't they know there's a war
there's a war a war going on down there

It was a storybook wedding in June
time stood still like a full moon
passion rose high in the primrose sky
the perfect picture of a young bride

With the struggles of the day-to-day
oh the anger that wrecks men's souls
and without the skills in human way
seeking violence the manly way
but violence it has no friends
not to women, girls or boy children

When the perfect family image dies again
some woman pays in all our names

Don't they know there's a war

Swirling of Her Coffee

The pattern of lace on the tablecloth
could hold her gaze for many a daze
she follows each thread
intricately led
trapped in a web
in the swirling of her coffee/swirling of her coffee

Memories are trapped
dreams run free
she plays with the patterned rim of gold
the antique cup
the spoon chimed and chinked
as she stirs
breaks the silence
in her apartment

The world went dead inside her head
try as she may she could never pluck herself away
the more she thinks the less she feels
her mounting fears erase the place
she'll arrive at/arrive at

She walks to the closet opens the door
stares at the minks she once wore
in those nights called remember

And her favourite song is a tune called forget
on the tip of her lips waiting to be expressed
a world so delicately held
in a motionless spell
and all could disappear in a flash

Memories are trapped
dreams run free
in an absurdity
in the swirling of her coffee/swirling of her coffee

a woman stirs her coffee
and the chiming of the spoon
the whirl of the moon
the stillness of her thoughts
so delicately held
in the swirling of her coffee/swirling of her coffee

no one wants her screams
no rescue teams
pluck her from her palliate dreams

memories are trapped
dreams run free
in an absurdity
in the swirling of her coffee/swirling of her coffee

Mrs

In the waiting room
a routine checkup
a technician came in
called me by what
she made my name
Mrs
I didn't answer but knowing
it was I, mumbled
and made my way
in a pace of my own
in a tempo earned
from struggle and long places
of silences

I no longer engage words
or meanings such as
Mistress
rhymes with distress
Miss
missed nothing
Mrs
misses rarely with words
Missus
miss us, ourselves
when we answer to words
others name us

de root of all language is impulse

Rasta in Court

Listen to the sound an' the beat of yu heart
Listen to the rebels an' the Rasta dem a talk
Listen to them chanting… listen to dem rapping
Listen to the shifting of the planet that is happening

The Rastaman check him bike
sey him haffi go down to Eglinton this night
ride him bike pon the sidewalk bright
bops to the left and weave to the right
dolly 'round the corner feeling very nice
'im ites green and gold flashing bold in the night
him hands off the handle bar of him bike
and before yu could sey "Hey Dreadie, everything alright?"
'im smash right into a policeman on patrol in the night

Oh what a fright   oh what a sight
Rastaman lying on top of a policeman with 'im bike
The policeman revive…jumpup hypnotized
and promptly arrest the Rastaman man
for riding 'im bicycle without any light

Rastaman reply
"I am one of Jah Jah children
I and I got my light which is Jah-guide
so, dem can't come arrest I and I
'cause in Babylon there's no night"

As the law would have it
them went to court
As Rasta luck would get it
jury dope
strict stiff courtroom full
judge keen and jury dutiful
The Rastaman decide to defend himself
and present him case in full

First him call himself as a witness
(hear wey him sey now, 'him is Jah witness');
"Ma light your honour is in I eye
If I ride my bicycle when I eye shut
I couldn't did see nothing
no matter if there was a thousand light 'pon I bike
When Jah give light him give I and I, I sight
And I eyes was open
So yu honour, dem can't come sey
I and I was riding without any light"

So the Judge sey, "... ah... ah let me try and get it straight
Mr. whats-yu-name... Rastafari You-and-you... If your eyes
were closed there would be darkness, no light. But your eyes
were open so...... so that meant you had your light...
Ah see... Then how come you run into the policeman with
your bike?"

"Because, yu honour," Rastaman replied, "as there is dark-
ness... there is light. And if the policeman did have 'im
light... him oulda did see I"

Guilty or not guilty   a jury must decide

"... And further more yu honour," Rastaman chides,
"Only one man can judge I and that is Jah Rastafari, Selassie I"

The jury returned split.   Verdict undecide
the judge had was to let the Rastaman slide
The policeman clutch him chest and started to cry

Rastaman jump 'pon him chariot of a bike
'im ites green and gold
flashing like a light
him a bob and a weave and hear him as him ride...
"Mi light beside mi liver... And mi light in mi eye...
can't check sey I mon Rasta guilty
when from Jah I and I get I guide!"
And off rode Rastaman to his contented life

And so the story goes... of a Rastaman, him bicycle and him light
... the judge it was said later resigned
went to live in the hills way up on high
And as for the policeman... he transferred to the day shift
in the Rosedale Heights...

Listen to the sound an' the beat of yu heart
Listen to the rebels an' the Rasta dem a talk
Listen to them chanting... listen to dem rapping
Listen to the shifting of the planet that is happening

Song for Newfoundland

The pace of unfolding Newfoundland's life
connects to my own
though I am Caribbean in North American clime
I could make Newfoundland my home

Language swirl of the Newfoundlander's roll
where syllables greet each other
as if long-lost cousins
hold and embrace slip   flip
and slide away
where word rhythms sway
make the voice rise   sing
twist and play

It is here in the family of heart rhythms
and soul beats
a great big wall-less place
where the letter "h" disappears
for a well deserved vacation
somewhere between language and music
in a mystical twilight haze
I found my connection
Newfoundland's soul

Fine Mary

(It was said she left the fine country
and walked right into the big city zoo)

She left the country for the city boom ba da ba ba da
she packed her suitcase she packed her boots
and headed east in her cowboy suit

You could say she got a bout of the terrified
thinking did she do it right
wondering if this was her demise
can't see quite what to do
all she knows she has to press on through
and find Mary find Mary find Mary

She got a job in a restaurant
serving up her country charm
now she works the double-shift
swings trays in her cowboy outfit

She missed her lover, her family
learned it the hard way
there's a price to be free
She never got her heart untuned
figured she could stay till June
but life you know has its own designs
keep on trucking and you'll do just fine
find Mary find Mary find Mary

If you hang a left 'round the corner down by the bay
you'll see Mary's little café
If you're down and out don't know what to say
Mary she'll say "How about trying my
get-up-stand-up soup?
Or sip from a bowl of my revolutionary brew"

Fine Mary fine Mary
you'll do just fine Mary
serving up that there menu

She left the country for the city boom ba da ba ba da
packed her suitcase packed her boots
headed east in her cowboy suit
and now she works the double-shift
swings trays in her cowboy outfit

Newfoundland's Magic
(on the road to Petty Harbour)

Glacial history bobs the shores
oceanic soup chunks and slushes
slaps the rugged Atlantic coast
sculptured mountains of polished snow
fine tuned by the wind
rise majestic and mystical
blue tinged
a gigantic ballerina's presence
on a watery stage

Icebergs quiet as tree trunks
stare upon the land as if recording
to wash away again
and sway with the waves
journeying into mists
a vaporous jig back to the liquid sea
taking the rhymes of Newfoundland
to other shores

Somewhere out at sea
in the Atlantic motion
Caribbean waves meet Newfoundland waters
exchange secrets
and bind us in a dance

In These Canadian Bones

In these Canadian bones
where Africa landed
and Jamaica bubble
inna reggae redstripe
and calypso proddings of culture
We are creating this very landscape
we walk on

My daughter sings opera
speaks perfect Canadian
And I dream in dialect
grown malleable by my Canadian tongue
of a world where all that matters is
the colour of love/compassion/heart
and music that grooves you

And I care about Québec
not just for Montréal
that pulsing city in heat
whose hips I want to stride
but for the tempo of language
stride and stridency in ownership of culture
not the hot air fascism
distinct of Bouchard
but the way they love jazz

And I thank the natives for this country
a guest on the planet
we all are

No Longer at Bat

if I were a baseball player
up at bat
when certain words came
I'd hold my bat away
let the ball fly
to wherever it will
and drop
with all its weight

a silent thud
that shatters

my eyes are no longer on a ball
that society or anyone else
throws me

the square root of impulse is language

poem for bp

vagina.

you had none
but it don't matter bp
cause tho u came through one
u never really left

it always pulled you back
sucked u in o
speaking a space

and u became a womb
birth a child of canadian culture
promise destruction of borders
in the turbulence of language

salacious syntax sinuations
and breath writing itself
a moist greening of what poetry could
and country o
your gospel of creativity

Billie Holiday

Oh Billie you lived in your drawl
sounds swirling out of black
rainbows splintering
through deceptions of greys
to your omniscient blues

so full of self
of music
in-your-face proud

passions burst into words
pride aches heartbeat
and slow defiance
note by note
Bessie's swing converges
Louis Armstrong blowing language
breaking words apart
scat scat scattering soul
all over art   all over american culture

Billie's lips giving shapes and hues to longings
meditation on deep spirit
on pain of being
elusive love
motions in the blood
fire and history from the bones
Billie's voice a poet's ease
and all that sass

Dem Days

Dem days oh dem days
dem days backa yard
oh de ole talk
an bus laugh
fi peas soup
a time when everything ripe
that is how mi like to remember home

but if it wasn't fa the fat one, the round one
the one dem who big and broad
and if it wasn't fa the tough head one dem
the one dem who scrawney
full a bad talk
box food outa mouth bark
the one dem whose puppa
work inna other people's yard

and if it wasn't fi the bwoy
wear im hand-mi-down shoes to the ground
and the girl whose mother wash and starch
her one frock till the cloth thin thru

and if it wasn't fa the one dem whose mother sell
inna the market
and the tarra one whose father try a ting ting
say him a sing sing

if it wasn't fa dem dey
accept ones just as dem stay
gwan galang share de likkle
dem have
nuh pop stylish like dem is big sinting

and if it wasn't fah them
bwoy! a tell yu
life a yard oulda did hard

an if it wasn't fa some of the olders
who sey pickney full a spirit and life
and must survive
jump and prance tackle new heights
and give respect regardless
and de people dem who expect
good things from yu
and all those who cheer yu on

and if it wasn't fi the friends who dedey
be dem same stellar self with apologies to no one

an if it wasn't fa the people dem
who when dem fight
mekup and love again
sinting and times
front and behind

dem people dey, mi sey
is the ones who mek life wut it
dem people dey, mi sey
wid little or nothing
squeeze soup outa rocks
mek yu feel whoever yu be
yu is not alone
yu can call fi dem gates yu own

a dem people dey mek mi remember home

cause the ones them who arrive
a school inna chauffeured car
dem oulda never did invite yu
a dem yard, Star
No! dem ouldn't even give yu time a day
ask yu how things stay

and if it wasn't fi the music
and the sighting up of things
and the good sinting
that come from the people deep within

if it wasn't for the gaddys,
grandmothers uncles and the aunts
cousins dems who check in
fill the void
make whole the parts

if it wasn't fa family and friends
and sis and brethren dem

and if it wasn't for the sunset
and the weather and the rain
the air soothe free to breathe
trees them for eyes to feast
and the sky wey nuh yet colonize

wi ouldn't did think sey yard soh sweet
no! wi ouldn't did think sey yard soh sweet

and if it wasn't for the place call home
a spirit that sets you apart but not alone
vibes and the niceness from inside
burn bright as the sun
although sometimes oppression clutch you
and frustration bubble deep down

and if it wasn't for that and all
mi ouldn't dida think fi member life
back a yard at all

and if it wasn't for the music
roaming street, early morning walks
river bath...
if it wasn't for the heat, breeze
rice and peas
sunday morning ackee and saltfish
easter bun with cheese
bulla, fritters, dumpling and sercy tea

and if it wasn't for the mango and the soursop
dasheen, naseberry, guineps, jimbilin,
star apple, guava, pineapple and coconut ice cream
mi ouldn't did member yard
no, not so much at all

and if it wasn't for the deep shining blackness
that be an ancestral drum   drum   / drum
and a river that run underground   ground / ground
knowing how we survive
with the music by wi side
and the drum
if it wasn't for this and all
bwoy a tell you
mi ouldn't did have love back a yard

and if it wasn't for the love
wi give one another
de light of the face of desire
that give the room a glint / glint
make mi think   think
lawd!!!
black people sweet sah

an if it wasn't for de beat of wi heart
that don't set itself from Africa apart
(in a these here foreign parts?)
wi oulda did lost

oh lawd!!!
wi oulda did lost

We Shall Take Our Freedom and Dance

They say times are hard but yu know what
yu gotta make it real
'cause whatever belongs to Caesar
belongs to the people

We shall take our freedom and dance
live the life we want
swing to the beat of our hearts
in a freedom chant
and dance

Got one life to live
no matter what they say or do
no one can live that life for you
so dance   dance

Take your life and live it
just the way you want
and dance   dance

And if someone doesn't like it
they can bite it   take a hike
go fly a kite   see a psychic
take a light trip on a spaceship
way out there
so dance   dance

We shall take our freedom and dance
and dance   and dance
da da da da da dance

We shall live the life we want
and dance
we shall take the joy from our dancing
to our world of understanding
and dance
swing to the beat of our hearts
live our freedom chants
and dance   and dance
and da da dada da dada
dance

Woman of Many Hands

The woman of many hands
holds geometry in her palm
conjures things with wings
and plays with the moon at night

Woman of many hands
inna the struggle long lang
holds a baby like the revolution
as a reminder

The woman of many hands
comes with a vision
plants her toil
with a sweet sedition

Woman of many hands
steals moments outside the clock
breathes a tide of silence
Brave as a rock rock rock rock

Woman of many hands
with an alchemist of a gaze
tends measly details
stirs the ingredient love
turns a house into a home
and that's not the magician side of her yet

The woman of many hands
loaned two to the clock
and wouldn't take them back
whether they ticked or they tocked

The woman of many hands
reaches out
grows another
when all the rest are busy

The woman of many hands
needs the world to be kind
needs a bouquet of songs
needs round hellos
sun beneath the skin

Woman of many hands
carries the revolution
close to her breast
like a newborn child

She feeds and cares for it
cleans its bum tends its misery
with no attention to fashion
or flavour of the month

She must guide it to itself
keep its dreams and visions nurtured
mission to be discovered
and fulfilled

Lest it stumbles and trips
over personal hardship/ships
and societal adversity
and becoming delinquent drifts

Phonological language: "hello...hello..."

But Oh!

it's true!
you have a long-standing craze
and play at immortality way too often
you believe in loving without mercy
I believe in love with no regret

when we are together   we deceive ourselves
that we are the moment

some days with you are like eternity
don't know when it begins
can see no end

but oh! oh oh
your smile provokes a poem in me
and I would love to make a revolution
with you

Chancing Rain

(woke up one morning   rushed to the mailbox
a postcard. From Arizona
The desert did you some good you said
then the phone calls...)

The sun persisted
golden streaks of spring
devours the last traces of winter's mists   mists
despite the weather report
and numerous forecasts for recession
we made plans for the sun and plenty

Silver streaks   joys   plate store windows
avenues of dullened pain
revenge had died inside of me

Overcast receded
golden glints memories   memories
a flood in the winter of my heart
I felt the crack
that precedes the thaw inside of me

I waited for you today at the corner of College and Bay

(the sun persisted
blazed inside of me
as I waited for you
hesistant and expectant)

You seized the odds from the weather report
always being a weather-watcher
and decided not to chance rain

(you decided not to chance rain)

Always believing what you believe is what you get
always believing what you get is what you need
always needing to believe that you're perfect
in your imperfection
always always always

I walked away today from the corner of College and Bay
not quite knowing what to believe or what to say

cities are like lovers
vast and rugged territory to explore
you can decide to live in it
or hit the road once more

The sun persisted
blazed inside of me as I waited for you today
at the corner of College and Bay

Soulmate

A book without words
nooooooooooooo plot
just expectations
and knowings
and being   there
with you

Soulmate

These Days a Gap

These days I contemplate a gap
a space where something used to be
but isn't anymore

These days I cry sometimes
when the rain whirs itself into my face

These days my mind is a feather
flirts with the softness of light
taunts the allure of a beckoning shade
and refuses to alight anywhere

These days I pray for a storm
that would outlast five storms
then blow itself into a clearing

These days I navigate a theory of self
in territories of intimate manoeuvres
careful to avoid crash-landings
unlit slippery alleys
mid-heart collisions
and slamming into mountains

These days whenever I fall
I just lie there
earth breathe into me
the wind smiling

Revolution from de Beat

Revolution from de drum
Revolution from de beat
Revolution from de heart
Revolution with de feet

De riddim and the heave and the sway of the beat
de rumblings and the tumblings down
to the dreams to the beat. To the impulse to be free
to the life that spring up in the heat   in the heat
in the pounding dance to be free
to bust open a window
crash upon a door
strip the crust of confinement
seep truth, through cracks
through the routing rhythms of the musical tracts   tracks

De sound of reggae music came on a wave of patter   patter
of deeply rooted internal chatter   chatter
on wings of riddim and melodies gone free
the bass strum the heart
the bass drum the heart beat
and the Rastaman pound! Bong bong   bong bong
beat them drums mon! Bong bong   bong bong

And de sound all around
and the voice
of impulse crafted into life burning darkness
of light
of days journeying through the night

of riddim pulse wails and dreams
and determination to be free
of sight
of a vision that ignites
of a musical bam-bam fling-down-baps get-up-stand-up jam!
A musical realignment of the planets
a joy and a singing for those on it

Liberation impulse
dig the colonialists' grave
crunch of the sixties
baton carried through civil rights flames
spirit of the hippies
signify new ways
the Black power five
the right-on jive
women raise banners for their rights
communities organize
and workers struggle for human rights   for human rights

De core of the African self
separated by four hundred years
ties blighted and nipped a   continental divide
and colonialist lies
a sip from the being of the African well
uncorked the primal African self
and woo...oosh woo...oo...oosh the well spring up
and a riddim let loose
and reggae music found us

It was the pulse in the Caribbean that echoed bright
a voice on a beat
squashed determination released
and the wondrous sighs of Black people once again rose high
from a little piece of rock called Jamaica
where Arawak and Carib bones lie
came a breath of resistance
of peace love and liberation
spread worldwide on the wings of its artists and shaman
the bass and drums prance like a winded fire
chenke ckenke chenke chenke of a guitar strum
songs of freedom
of spirit
of love
of redemption

Revolution from de drum
Revolution from de beat
Revolution from de heart
Revolution with de feet
Ah revolution

The mind seeks no permission
The poem doesn't ask for approval

Digitize This

Flickers across my screen
surf and sail
window to open sea

I am fingers
taps on a keyboard
letters on a screen
u receive me digitized

I in another room wash dishes
while u download
slide through my printer
bare softworn soul
over my buffed wood floor

In the Beginning...

Before there was memory, before "In the Beginning" everything was the same and the same and the same. And we yearned as one for difference. But we were one and the same and everything was just the same.

The same and the same and the same.

"In the Beginning" is how we described it when we first created God. The first time we remembered. The place where memory starts when we relinquished the rigidity of sameness. Memory starts here because the human mind can only remember by the experience of contrast. Before difference, humankind has no memory.

We created God to ease the monotony. This was our first human act of art. We gave God the ultimate responsibility for creating and for all things. This was how we first gave in to the possibility of difference, of motion, of flow — letting go the rigidity of sameness. This possibility produced free will. And God said "This is good". This was God's first action — to speak — to say "This is good."

And God felt good.

And these words and God's emotions of feeling good created motion. And this motion we call time. And we moved for the first time for the sheer effort of imitating God. And God called our motion dance. And our dancing was rhythmic and created the waves on which our voices rode and the movement of our voices on these waves created music. And the first organic life appeared on the downbeat of a song.

We said to each other, "We created God and that gave us possibilities. Possibilities made us move, movement made us dance, our dancing gave us music and music made new life.

For the first time we saw old and we saw new and saw that we were old. So we say to this God, "All things old, make them new."

And God said, "I don't make things new. That's your job. My job is to create difference. That's the job of God."

And we said, "We hate difference!"

And God replied, "Then how about just saving yous from yourselves?"

And we said, "Tacky, tacky, tacky. Had we known you were bringing your own agenda to the job, we would have made this a temporary position with a probationary period and possible renewal only on mutual agreement of the parties."

God said, "Too late now. Our job agreement has locked us in forever. We are going to have to tough this one out."

So we said, "Shucks! In that case we'll need to get you a job description quick because the next thing you know you'll be doing anything you darned well please."

And God said, "I feel a little bit of distrust developing here. What you need to understand is that I do what God does. Not what I darned well please."

On the way to creating a job description for God, we experienced the first possibility of dissent. At first we formed a committee, but everyone now knowing feelings of distrust, wanted to ensure that their opinion had the same prominence as every other, so we became a collective. This process went on for millennia. Everyone was giving their input, making sure details and conceivable eventualities were covered. Then there were changes and discussions and debates and arguments and not everyone could agree on every single point. People argued over why we even needed God in the first place. Some argued that they could do the job. On their prodding, a sub-committee was struck to work out a compromise delineating lines of accountability once the God thing was settled. Sometimes people forgot what it was they were trying to do. Some didn't like the way others presented. Some went off and had wars with those who didn't agree with them .

And finally someone said, "God has to serve my individual, unique needs or else why would I have a God."

And another said, "Look, we have to get on with it. God needs to get on with the business of being God."

Another said, "I've got my own job description for God. Why don't we all write our own."

And so we did. Each and every one. At the end of the process each person had fashioned God's job description to his or her own liking.

And God said, "You can make any kind of job description you want. When it comes down to it, I can only do what God does. Nothing more and nothing less."

And we laughed and said, "We'll see!"

And that was in the beginning.